April 1985

To Malcolm, with love
and best wishes for
a very happy birthday.

Andrew, Margaret,
Jacob, Dominic + Johanna.

CONSTANTINE THE GREAT

A. B. (BANJO) PATERSON

CONSTANTINE THE GREAT

Illustrated by Robert Lovett

Lansdowne
Sydney • Auckland • London • New York

Design: Pam Brewster
Published by Lansdowne, Sydney
a division of RPLA Pty Limited
176 South Creek Road, Dee Why West, N.S.W., Australia, 2099
First published 1984

Produced in Australia by the Publisher
Typeset in Australia by Savage & Co., Brisbane
Printed by Tien Mah Litho Printing (Pte) Ltd
2 Jalan Jentera Jurong Singapore 22

National Library of Australia Cataloguing-in-Publication Data
Paterson, A. B. (Andrew Barton), 1864–1941.
Constantine the Great.

For children.
ISBN 0 7018 1804 2.

1. Horses — Juvenile fiction. I. Lovett, Robert.
II. Title.

A823′.2

Arrival at 'Limestone'

The thoroughbred mares in their own exclusive paddock at Limestone stud were a very aristocratic lot, and as keen on their own dignity and precedence as a lot of patrician dowagers in a Court drawing-room: consequently, they were very much upset when a strange horse was turned in among them one bright December morning, without their permission being asked or their desires considered in any way whatever.

You must understand that these highly pedigreed ladies all figured in the pages of the *Stud Book*, which is the *Debrett's Peerage* of the Turf world, and they knew each other's pedigrees and relationships away back into the days of Charles I. Not a horse could win an important race in any part of the world and no mare could produce a Derby winner, but what such of the Limestone ladies as were related to the new celebrity became very proud and arrogant, and those who were not related became jealous — very jealous indeed.

Being a lot of highly bred dowagers, they were divided into as many cliques and coteries as the countesses and duchesses in a Mayfair drawing-room, and the credentials of any new arrival were very closely scanned before she was admitted to any of the more exclusive circles.

'That mare,' a dowager countess would say, on considering the pedigree of a new arrival, 'of course I shall call on her, but I really couldn't make a friend of her. My dear, do you know that her family haven't won a really big race for three generations?'

Besides an infinite number of smaller coteries, there were two clear-cut social sets among the mares — those born in England, and those born in Australia.

The English mares did not actually patronise the others, but they just tolerated them, and on Derby Day the English mares got together and talked about Epsom and Newmarket till the other mares could hardly bear it: and a pert young Australian mare, after listening to as much of this conversation as she could stand, said, 'The Epsom Derby! That's the race where they go up and down hills, isn't it, like our stockhorses go after cattle?' a remark that was passed over in a kind of pitying silence. But in spite of their bickering among themselves they presented a united front against all outsiders, and they looked upon any horse not in the *Stud Book* in much the same way as a duchess would look upon the bride of a costermonger.

And so, on this beautiful December day, a strange horse was actually being turned into their paddock, a big gaunt bay horse with hair on his fetlocks, a plain head and spur marks on his ribs: a horse that looked as though he ought to be carrying a general at the head of an army, so strong and resolute was his appearance, and so kind and intelligent was his eye; but the hair on his fetlocks, the spur marks on his ribs, and the plainness of his head decided the mares that he could not be a thoroughbred — perhaps something very near it, but not quite born in the purple. So they decided to ignore the intruder, and they cast calm supercilious glances at him as he strolled past them on his way to the river to get a drink.

The two men who had brought him to the paddock stood chatting by the rails. The mares knew one of them well enough, for the tall man with the heavy moustache and the slow soft way of speaking was Gordon Macallister, owner of the Limestone stud, and he was a personal friend of every mare in the paddock. He visited them nearly every day, he looked after them when they were sick and a word from him in praise of one of the foals was enough to make that foal's mother proud and joyful for a week.

The keen-eyed little man with the quick, staccato way of speaking was unknown to the mares and they put him down as not much class anyway; if they had known that he was Ike Heronshaw, the greatest trainer of the day, they would have been more impressed.

'Well, Ike,' said Macallister, 'this is the best I can do for you. No one goes through this paddock, and no one would dream of looking for him among my crack mares and foals. Why does his owner want him planted?'

'He's broke.'

'Broke! I thought he had plenty of money.'

'So he did have. But he wanted more, so he bought half the wool in Australia and shipped it and struck a misere hand. He's got no ready money, y'understand, and his creditors are after him, and if they can get hold of this horse they'll sell him by order of the Court. But the market's risin' and if he can hold on for a few weeks he'll be all right again. That's why he wants this horse out of the road.'

'I see. But I'm taking a risk putting him in with my mares and foals. I wouldn't dream of doing it for anybody but you. Is he quiet?'

'Quiet! You could bowl hedgehogs at his hind legs all day and he wouldn't kick at 'em. Your daughter could ride him, so then nobody would tumble to it that he is anything more than an ordinary hack. What I'm afraid of is that he might cripple himself if he gets galloping about with these foals.'

'That's what you're afraid of, is it? Well, what about me, taking the risk of turning a stranger into this paddock? He might set the whole lot racing for their lives! If I'll chance my mares and foals, you've got to chance your horse. If I put him anywhere else, somebody's sure to see him and you'll have the bailiffs after him.'

With that, the two men rode away to the homestead and the mares were left to size up the intruder.

Possibly the most aristocratic mare in the paddock was Lady Susan, a descendant of the great St Simon, and with so many other celebrated relatives that her position was almost unchallengeable. True, she was Australian-born, but her grandsire had won the English Derby and she herself had won the Australian Oaks, and what was more important, her foals had won two Derbies and a Melbourne Cup. The English mares might affect to despise Australian races, but any foal from Lady Susan was worth five thousand guineas as it stood on its delicate little hoofs alongside her in the paddock. The English mares might talk about Epsom and Newmarket, but none of their foals averaged five thousand guineas, so there was no more to be said: all the mares waited for a lead from Lady Susan in most matters, but in regard to this new horse they thought they were on safe ground in criticising him.

The chorus was led off by Cat's Cradle, a young and pert Australian mare who was inclined to give herself airs because her full sister

had won the last big race for two-year-old fillies by three lengths in very fast time. She was addicted to slang and after looking the newcomer over in a very supercilious way she gave a horse laugh, which is a kind of internal laugh that you can't see.

'Girls,' she said, 'what have we here? Pipe the marks of the harpoons on his ribs, and the whiskers on his fetlocks! I'll bet he's a winner — the winner of the Big Scrub Handicap with the first prize a bees' nest. After you've won the race, they show you the bees' nest in a tree, and you have to cut the tree down and rob the nest for yourself.'

Meanwhile the English mares were muttering among themselves such remarks as 'preposterous', 'wouldn't be tolerated in England', 'you never know what to expect in this extraordinary country,' being faintly heard above the singing of Featherbrain, an English mare who was apt to be a bit hysterical, who screamed to her foal and set off up the paddock as hard as she could split, but finding that none of the others followed her, returned in a shamefaced way to the mob.

All this time old Lady Susan had said nothing until her foal, who was quite an important person, for he was expected to fetch at least six thousand guineas at auction, went up to her and said, 'Mother, can I go and speak to the new horse? He seems so lonely, and none of the others will go near him.'

'Yes,' she said, 'you can go. I seem to see a likeness in that horse to somebody I used to know. I think I must have raced against his mother at some time or other. You mustn't say anything rude to him about the hair on his fetlocks, for sometimes that comes to us from the old English horses that were in the pedigrees hundreds of years before the Arabs were ever brought into England. Just be civil to him, and if he tells you anything come back and tell me,' — for even the greatest ladies are not above a little curiosity.

Without the slightest hesitation, Lady Susan's foal marched up to the newcomer and gave him the usual Australian salutation, 'Good day. It looks very dry, doesn't it?'

The stranger, who appeared to be a rough and ready sort of person, said, 'Yes, it's dry all right: and who may you be, young fellow?'

To which the foal, who had a great idea of his own importance though he was only a few months old, answered without any trepidation, 'I'm Lady Susan's foal. Perhaps you've heard of my full brother Gaslight?'

'Gaslight!' said the stranger. 'Why I ran against —' and here he stopped as though about to say too much. 'I ran against a stone coming up, and bruised my heel a bit. But look here, young fellow, it doesn't matter what you are full brother to. The thing is, can you gallop yourself? The Judge don't place any horse first because he's full brother to something, you know.'

'Oh, yes, I know that. But I can go a bit, and when the foals all get together for our gallop round the paddock this evening, you can see me travel. Did you ever do any racing yourself?'

'Oh yes, young fellow, I've raced a bit: not as much as some and more than others. The less you talk about what you can do in racing the better for you, you understand. The handicapper might hear you, and you'd never get the weight off. But I'll watch you go round this evening, and I might be able to give you a wrinkle or two that will do you some good when your time comes to go to the barrier.'

That evening when the foals gathered for their customary sprint round the paddock, the stranger watched them for a while and then tossed up his head and set after them, going in surprising fashion, his great strides eating up the ground, while the foals with their little nostrils distended and their little hoofs rattling on the stony ridges strove valiantly for the lead. The Featherbrain mare got very excited and said, 'Look, look, he'll kill the foals', to which Lady Susan, who

had picked up some hard sayings in the training stables, replied, 'Shut your head! The foals are all right.'

You see, her foal was well in front and going like a champion.

After the gallop Lady Susan's foal strolled over to the stranger, expecting to get all sorts of compliments, but the stranger was not of the gushing type. 'Very fair,' he said. 'Very fair, but look here, youngster, when you first jump off, don't make too big a jump. It's all right with nothing on your back, but when you've got a jockey there, too big a jump will unbalance him. Just take half a stride as you move out of the barrier, and get the weight on your back under way. Then get down to it and deal it out to 'em all you know. Give my compliments to your mother and tell her I know all about her. Everybody on the Turf knows all about Lady Susan.'

The Fire

That was the year of the big bushfire, the fire that swept up the river from a hundred miles south, burning all before it. It had been a great season, and the long grass and thistles on the flats were as dry as tinder, and the wind brought the fire along in great leaps, the burning cinders being carried by the wind from the dry trees to start fresh fires half a mile ahead. When the breeze brought the first scent of the burning gum leaves, and the clouds of smoke appeared over the distant hills, the mares gathered themselves and their foals together, sniffing with pointed ears at the new terror — something of which none of them had had any experience whatever.

It so happened that Macallister was away from the head station that day, and he only arrived in his car as night fell, bringing with him his daughter, Jean, a fourteen-year-old girl with just as much interest in the horses as Macallister himself. She had been riding ever since she could remember anything, ever since the days when she was carried as a baby in front of her father's saddle.

Springing from the car, Macallister dragged a bridle out of the tonneau, and walking in a quiet, matter-of-fact way he went up to the stranger and slipped the bridle on him, talking to him in a soothing voice all the time. Then he led him up to the car and told his daughter what she must do.

'Jean,' he said, 'that fire will be here in ten minutes and all I've got in the world is in these mares and foals. There's only one thing that can save them, and that is this horse. This is Constantine the Great, the horse that won both the Sydney and Melbourne Derbies and the Melbourne Cup. You'll have to ride him bareback, for there's no time to go and get a saddle, but they say he's very quiet. Now listen to what I've got to tell you.

'As soon as I let the mares and foals out of this paddock, they'll go like mad things all over the bush, and half of them will be crippled or killed in the darkness: but if you can keep ahead of them for the first mile, they'll follow you and you can lead them up to the big bald hill where there's no grass and no timber. When you get them there, try and keep them there — do your best anyhow. They'll be pretty tired by that time and if you keep on riding round and round, and calling out to them in the darkness they may follow you and it may save the lot.

'And now there's another thing. There's that gate at the Two Mile. You'll have no time to stop and open it or the mares will scatter all over the place. Run him right slap into it, and send it flying. It opens in the middle and his weight will smash it like paper. Don't stop for anything and don't look behind you. The mares will follow you through the gate and the main thing is to keep ahead of them the first mile. If there's a horse in the world that can keep ahead of those thoroughbred mares with nothing on their backs, this is the one. I did not want him here, but it looks as if he might save us.

'As soon as I get you away, I'll go up to the house and tell your mother to hide in the river if the fire comes, and then I'll go back to try and save that old crippled woman down in the hut on the flat.'

Even as he spoke a red glare showed down at the bend of the river and the mares grew terrified. Swinging the girl on to the big horse's back, he led him towards the gate, patting him on the neck, and talking to him.

'Old man,' he said, 'you're running for a big stake tonight. Bigger than the Melbourne Cup. There's a hundred thousand pounds of money in these mares and there's my little girl's life. It's up to you to save them, so now go to it like a thoroughbred.'

By this time they had reached the gate, the big horse walking quite unconcerned, while the terrified mares crowded behind him.

Giving his daughter a hurried kiss, Macallister threw the gate open, and with the big horse in front, the wild cavalcade swept away into the darkness.

For the first half mile Jean knew nothing but the great swinging strides of the horse beneath her, the dimly seen stretch of track in front, and behind her the roaring of hundreds of hoofs and the mares whinnying and calling to their foals. If she came off, or if the big horse made a false step in the darkness and came down, she would be trodden flat in an instant by the terrified rush of the mares behind her: but there was a wild exhilaration in the ride that ban-

ished all thought of fear. Constantine the Great lay down to work without fear or excitement, for it was nothing new to him to hear the drumming of a field of horses behind him. Some instinct inherited from his Arab ancestors made him reach out and clear in his stride the little waterways that crossed the track. Once or twice in the headlong flight the girl's knee grazed perilously against the trees, and more than once she had to lie flat down on his neck to avoid being swept off by an overhanging branch: but still the great machine-like stride swept him along in front of the mares, and still they followed in close formation at his heels. After a while the pace slackened and Jean was able to sit up and call out to the mares, who knew her voice and answered her with shrill neighs: but the pace was still fast enough to make any delay risky and Jean knew that if she stopped to open the Two Mile gate the mares would probably swing on down the fence into the darkness and smash themselves up in the scrub.

Having got so far in safety, her spirits rose and she amused herself by talking to the big horse as they swept along.

'There's a gate ahead of us,' she said, 'and you've got to smash it or these mares and foals will be killed. Will you do it for me? Don't jump it, or I'll very likely come off, for I'm not very good at jumping fences barebacked, and if the mares follow you over it, that will be the end of me.'

Luckily, the gate was hidden under the shadow of some trees, and the big horse was on it before he saw it.

With no time to jump he gave a snort of defiance and raced straight into it.

Smash! The two by four hardwood battens were splintered like matches under the weight of the blow, and without pause or hesitation he swept on while the mares crowded and crushed through the gap that he had left. So instantaneous had been the smash that Jean had hardly been shifted on her precarious perch, but with each stride that the big horse took she felt something moist on her hands. She was puzzled to think what it could be, but at last she realised that the horse had cut himself rather badly on the gate and that his blood was splashing up on to her hands and clothes. For the first time in that wild ride she felt utterly miserable, but there was nothing that could be done about it so she held her course through the rough timber for the Bald Hill.

Arriving at the hill, she found that an advanced wing of the fire had nearly cut her off, and everything was red flames, smoke, and confusion. In a sort of sanctuary on top of the hill, all sorts of bush animals had gathered, wallabies and kangaroos bewildered with terror racing madly round and round, while rabbits with their fur on fire rushed screaming across the open. A mob of emus, all fear of mankind forgotten, trotted up to her and almost stuck their heads in her face as though asking for guidance. Coming up at their ungainly trot, they had cut the mob of mares in two, and for a moment it looked as though one wing of the mares would lose their heads and race into the scrub; but just as things hung in the balance a foal trotted towards her from the outlying mob, his mother followed him, and in another moment all the mares had gathered together again.

By the light of the burning trees Jean recognised the foal that had so unexpectedly come to her help at a critical moment. 'Why,' she said, 'it's Silas! And he seems to know this horse! Aren't you frightened, Silas?' But Silas, with his small nostrils sniffing the smoke, was quite at his ease, and appeared to think that Providence would hesitate before destroying a gentleman of his quality.

Ringed with smoke and fire, and hampered by terrified wild animals, Jean rode backwards and forwards through the night, keeping the mares together and vainly trying to see what injury her mount had sustained. She dared not get off the horse lest she should never be able to get on again, but as daylight broke she was able to see a big raw gash across his chest from which the blood still welled and, overcome with weariness and excitement, she burst into tears.

A few hours later a big gaunt horse with bloodstained chest and forelegs, and ridden by an inexpressibly weary little girl, led the Limestone mares back to the homestead. Here she found the lucerne paddocks had saved the house from destruction, and after receiving the frantically excited greetings of her father and mother, her first thought was of the injury that her horse had sustained at the gate. After examination her father pronounced it only superficial, and it was a thankful girl that tumbled into bed to sleep off the recollections of the night amidst the fire.

When things had settled down a bit in the horse paddock once more, Lady Susan marched up to the stranger and said, 'We have to thank you for saving our lives. Do you mind telling me your name? These English ladies and myself are now of the opinion that you must be a far more important person than you look.'

'Well ma'am,' he said, 'I have a name all right. Such as it is you may have heard it, for they call me Constantine the Great. As for importance, well, I've won some races and I've lost others. I've raced against some of your foals and you want to look after that little fellow you have now, for a gamer bit of stuff I never saw.'

When the mares discovered who he was, there was great excitement in hunting over his pedigree, and it was found that he was first cousin to fifteen of them, and was more or less distantly related to every mare in the paddock. It took them several days to hunt out all the relationships.

A few months later the leading newspaper starred the item: 'Constantine the Great has come back to work, and appears to be in great fettle except that his chest is disfigured by a scar which he no doubt sustained while playing about in the paddock. It does not give him any trouble and he is certain to add to his already imposing record of wins.'